Starfall Sing-Along

Volume 1

A book of lyrics with audio CD.

Starfall®

ISBN: 978-1-59577-091-2

Starfall Education

P.O. Box 359, Boulder, CO 80306

Table of Contents

1 A Hunting We Will Go

A hunting we will go
A hunting we will go
We'll catch a fox and put him in a box
And then we'll let him go

A hunting we will go
A hunting we will go
We'll catch a fish and put him on a dish
And then we'll let him go

A hunting we will go
A hunting we will go
We'll catch a bear and cut his hair
And then we'll let him go

A hunting we will go
A hunting we will go
We'll catch a pig and dance a jig
And then we'll let him go

2 Alphabet Song

A - B - C - D - E - F - G
H - I - J - K - L - M - N - O - P
Q - R - S, T - U - V
W - X, Y and Z;
Now I know my ABCs
Next time won't you sing with me?

America the Beautiful 3

O beautiful for spacious skies
For amber waves of grain
For purple mountain majesties
Above the fruited plain
America! America!
God shed his grace on thee
And crown thy good with brotherhood
From sea to shining sea

Backpack Bear's ABCs 4

Backpack Bear runs in the door
And hunts for letters on the floor
He grabs them quick and hides them well
Where he hides them, he won't tell
Off he goes to wait some more
For you to find them on the floor!

5 Backpack Is a Little Bear

Backpack is a little bear
Little bear, little bear
Backpack is a little bear
Whose fur is soft and brown

Backpack's playing hide and seek
Hide and seek, hide and seek
Backpack's playing hide and seek
Where can that bear be found?

Backpack is at school today
School today, school today
Backpack is at school today
To learn the reading rules

He will make you laugh and play
Laugh and play, laugh and play
He will make you laugh and play
Yes! Backpack is at school

Down by the A-B-Sea

Down by the A-B-Sea
Where the coconuts grow
There is a place
I want to go
But if I do
My teacher might say:
Did you see A and B or C and D
Up in a tree?

Down by the A-B-Sea
Where the coconuts grow
There is a place
I want to go
But if I do
My teacher might say:
Did you see E and F, G, H or I
Up near the sky?

Down by the A-B-Sea
Where the coconuts grow
There is a place
I want to go
But if I do
My teacher might say:
Did you see J and K or L and M
Joining them?

Down by the A-B-Sea
Where the coconuts grow
There is a place
I want to go
But if I do
My teacher might say:
Did you see N and O or P and Q
Following you?

Down by the A-B-Sea
Where the coconuts grow
There is a place
I want to go
But if I do
My teacher might say:
Did you see R and S and T and U
In front of you?

Down by the A-B-Sea
Where the coconuts grow
There is a place
I want to go
But if I do
My teacher might say:
Did you see V and W, X, Y, Z
Up in a tree?

7 Every Day Is Earth Day

Our big Earth needs cleaning, cleaning
Our big Earth needs cleaning now
Pick up the litter!
Plant a tree!
Now our Earth is better you see!

Our big Earth needs cleaning, cleaning
Our big Earth needs cleaning now

8 Five Little Bears

One little bear
Wondering what to do
Along came another
Then there were two!

Two little bears
Climbing up a tree
Along came another
Then there were three!

Three little bears
Ate an apple core
Along came another
Then there were four!

Four little honey bears
Found honey in a hive
Along came another
And then there were five!

Five Little Chickadees

Five little chickadees
Pecking at the door
One flew away and
Then there were four

Four little chickadees
Sitting in a tree
One flew away and
Then there were three

Three little chickadees
Looking at you
One flew away and
Then there were two

Two little chickadees
Sitting in the sun
One flew away and
Then there was one

One little chickadee
Left all alone
He flew away and
Then there were none

10 Five Little Monkeys

Five little monkeys
Jumping on the bed
One fell off and bumped his head
Mother called the doctor and the doctor said,
"No more monkeys jumping on the bed!"

Four little monkeys
Jumping on the bed
One fell off and bumped his head
Mother called the doctor and the doctor said,
"No more monkeys jumping on the bed!"

Three little monkeys
Jumping on the bed
One fell off and bumped his head
Mother called the doctor and the doctor said,
"No more monkeys jumping on the bed!"

Two little monkeys
Jumping on the bed
One fell off and bumped his head
Mother called the doctor and the doctor said,
"No more monkeys jumping on the bed!"

One little monkey
Jumping on the bed
He fell off and bumped his head
Mother called the doctor and the doctor said,
"Get those monkeys back to bed!"

Georgie Porgie

Georgie Porgie puddin' and pie
Kissed the girls and made them cry
When the boys came out to play
Georgie Porgie ran away

Head, Shoulders, Knees and Toes

Head, shoulders, knees and toes, knees and toes
Head, shoulders, knees and toes, knees and toes and
Eyes and ears and mouth and nose
Head, shoulders, knees and toes, knees and toes

Fingers, elbows, hips and ankles, hips and ankles
Fingers, elbows, hips and ankles, hips and ankles
Hair and cheeks and chin and neck
Fingers, elbows, hips and ankles, hips and ankles

(repeat 3 times, getting faster each time)

13 Hens Are Marching

The hens are marching round and round
Hurrah! Hurrah!

The hens are marching round and round
Hurrah! Hurrah!

The hens are marching round and round
Words that rhyme with hen*, Sit Down!

And we'll all go marching round
Until
We all sit down!

(* The word "hen" is sung "pet" in the
second verse, and "red" in the third verse.)

Hey Diddle Diddle 14

Hey diddle diddle
The cat and the fiddle
The cow jumped over the moon (He did?)
The little dog laughed to see such sport
And the dish ran away with the spoon

Hickory, Dickory, Dock 15

Hickory, dickory, dock
Zac ran up the clock
The clock struck one
Zac ran down!
Hickory, dickory, dock

Hickory, dickory, dock
Zac slept by the clock
The clock struck four
He ran out the door!
Hickory, dickory, dock

Hickory, dickory, dock
Zac ran up the clock
The clock struck noon
He's here too soon!
Hickory, dickory, dock

16 Humpty-Dumpty

Humpty-Dumpty sat on a wall
Humpty-Dumpty had a great fall
All the King's horses and all the King's men
Couldn't put Humpty together again

17 Jam

Jam on my head (Your head?)
Jam on my toes (Your toes?)
Jam on my hands
Jam on my nose

Laughing and a-licking
Having me a time
Jam on my belly
But I like it fine

Jam is my favorite food
When I'm in a jelly mood
I can never get enough
Of that yummy, gummy stuff

Jam on my knees
Jam in my hair
Jam on my tail
Jam everywhere

Laughing and a-licking
Having me a time
Boy I am so sticky
But I like it fine

Jam is my favorite food
When I'm in a jelly mood
I can never get enough
Of that yummy, gummy stuff

Little Plant

In the heart of a seed
Buried down so deep
A little plant
Lay fast asleep

    "Awake," said the sun
    "Come up through the earth"
    "Awake," said the rain
    "We are giving you birth"

The little plant heard
With a happy sigh
And pointed his petals
Up to the sky

19 Looby Loo

Here we go looby loo
Here we go looby light
Here we go looby loo
All on a Saturday night

I put my right hand in
I take my right hand out
I give my hand
 a shake, shake, shake
And turn myself about

Here we go looby loo
Here we go looby light
Here we go looby loo
All on a Saturday night

I put my left hand in
I take my left hand out
I give my hand
 a shake, shake, shake
And turn myself about

Here we go looby loo
Here we go looby light
Here we go looby loo
All on a Saturday night

I put my right foot in
I take my right foot out
I give my foot
 a shake, shake, shake
And turn myself about

I put my left foot in
I take my left foot out
I give my foot
 a shake, shake, shake
And turn myself about

Here we go looby loo
Here we go looby light
Here we go looby loo
All on a Saturday night

I put my little head in
I take my little head out
I give my head
 a shake, shake, shake
And turn myself about

I put my whole self in
I take my whole self out
I give myself
 a shake, shake, shake
And turn myself about

Here we go looby loo
Here we go looby light
Here we go looby loo
All on a Saturday
All on a Saturday
All on a Saturday
All on a Saturday
All on a Saturday night

Mary Had a Little Lamb

Mary had a little lamb
Little lamb, little lamb
Mary had a little lamb
Its fleece was white as snow

    And everywhere that Mary went
    Mary went, Mary went
    And everywhere that Mary went
    The lamb was sure to go

It followed her to school one day
School one day, school one day
It followed her to school one day
Which was against the rules

    It made the children laugh and play
    Laugh and play, laugh and play
    It made the children laugh and play
    To see a lamb at school

21 Months of the Year

January, February, March and April
May and June, July and August
September, October, November, December
These are the months of the year

January
February
March
and April
May
and June
July
and August
September
October
November
December

These are the months of the year

18

Mulberry Bush

Here we go round the mulberry bush
The mulberry bush, the mulberry bush
Here we go round the mulberry bush
So early in the morning

This is the way we wash our clothes
Wash our clothes, wash our clothes
This is the way we wash our clothes
So early Monday morning

This is the way we iron our clothes
Iron our clothes, iron our clothes
This is the way we iron our clothes
So early Tuesday morning

This is the way we mend our clothes
Mend our clothes, mend our clothes
This is the way we mend our clothes
So early Wednesday morning

This is the way we sweep the floor
Sweep the floor, sweep the floor
This is the way we sweep the floor
So early Thursday morning

This is the way we scrub the floor
Scrub the floor, scrub the floor
This is the way we scrub the floor
So early Friday morning

This is the way we bake our bread
Bake our bread, bake our bread
This is the way we bake our bread
So early Saturday morning

23 Old MacDonald Had a Farm

Old MacDonald had a farm, "a-e-i-o-u"
And on his farm he had a rat, "a-e-i-o-u"
With an "/a/-/a/" here and an "/a/-/a/" there
Here an "/a/" there an "/a/" everywhere an "/a/-/a/"
Old MacDonald had a farm, "a-e-i-o-u"

Old MacDonald had a farm, "a-e-i-o-u"
And on his farm he had a hen, "a-e-i-o-u"
With an "/e/-/e/" here and an "/e/-/e/" there
Here an "/e/" there an "/e/" everywhere an "/e/-/e/"
Old MacDonald had a farm, "a-e-i-o-u"

Old MacDonald had a farm, "a-e-i-o-u"
And on his farm he had a pig, "a-e-i-o-u"
With an "/i/-/i/" here and an "/i/-/i/" there
Here an "/i/" there an "/i/" everywhere an "/i/-/i/"
Old MacDonald had a farm, "a-e-i-o-u"

Old MacDonald had a farm, "a-e-i-o-u"
And on his farm he had a fox, "a-e-i-o-u"
With an "/o/-/o/" here and an "/o/-/o/" there
Here an "/o/" there an "/o/" everywhere an "/o/-/o/"
Old MacDonald had a farm, "a-e-i-o-u"

Old MacDonald had a farm, "a-e-i-o-u"
And on his farm he had a duck, "a-e-i-o-u"
With an "/u/-/u/" here and an "/u/-/u/" there
Here an "/u/" there an "/u/" everywhere an "/u/-/u/"
Old MacDonald had a farm, "a-e-i-o-u"

One, Two, Buckle My Shoe 24

One, two, buckle my shoe
Three, four, shut the door
Five, six, pick up sticks
Seven, eight, lay 'em straight
Nine, ten, Peg the Hen!

Open Them, Shut Them 25

Open, shut them, open, shut them
Give a little clap

Open, shut them, open, shut them
Lay them in your lap

Creep them, creep them
Slowly creep them
Right up to your chin
Open up your little mouth
But do not let them in!

26 Peas Porridge Hot

Peas porridge hot, peas porridge cold
Peas porridge in a pot nine days old

Some like it hot, some like it cold
Some like it in a pot nine days old

27 Peg and Gus

Peg the Hen took a walk one day
In the very best of weather

Along came Gus the Duck
And they both talked together

Cluck Cluck Cluck!
Quack Quack Quack!
Cluck Cluck Cluck!
Quack Quack Quack!
Cluck Cluck Cluck!
Quack Quack Quack!
Cluck Cluck Cluck!
Quack Quack Quack!

Goodbye, Goodbye
Goodbye, Goodbye

And they both walked back

Short-a Song 28

Listen to the short-a sound
/a/, /a/, /a/, /a/, /a/

The /a/ in "cat" the /a/ in "rat"
Make the short-a sound
/a/, /a/, /a/, /a/, /a/!

Short-e Song 29

Ed the elephant likes red eggs
/e/ /e/, /e/ /e/
Ed the elephant likes red eggs
/e/ /e/, /e/ /e/

Ed the elephant likes red eggs
He rolls them with his heavy legs

The short-e makes its very own sound
/e/ /e/, /e/ /e/

30 Short-i Song

The big hit went into the mitt
Can you hear short-i in it?

The big hit went into the mitt
Can you hear short-i in it?

31 Short-o Song

I know a fox who had a box
and loved the sound of /o/, /o/
Fox, fox, on a box
Fox, fox, on a box
Fox, fox, on a box
And that's the /o/ in "fox," /o/!

32 Short-u Song

The "u" in "Gus" goes /u/, /u/, /u/
/u/, /u/, /u/
/u/, /u/, /u/

The "u" in "Gus" goes /u/, /u/, /u/
Gus the Duck!

Take Me Out to the Ball Game 33

Take me out to the ball game
Take me out with the crowd
Buy me some peanuts and cracker jacks
I don't care if I never get back

Let me root, root, root for the home team
If they don't win it's a shame
For it's ONE, TWO, THREE strikes you're out
At the old ball game

Teddy Bear Says, "Thank You" 34

Teddy Bear, Teddy Bear
Say "Thank you"
Teddy Bear, Teddy Bear
Say "Please" too

> Teddy Bear, Teddy Bear
> Share your ball
> Teddy Bear, Teddy Bear
> Be nice to all

Teddy Bear, Teddy Bear
Raise your hand
Teddy Bear, Teddy Bear
Quietly stand

> Teddy Bear, Teddy Bear
> Walk, don't run
> Teddy Bear, Teddy Bear
> Have some fun!

35 The Clever Hen

I had a little hen
The prettiest ever seen
She washed up the dishes
And kept the house clean

She went to the mill
To fetch me some flour
And always got home
In less than an hour

She worked very hard
To bake me my bread
We ate by the fire
And then went to bed

Today Is Monday

Today is Monday
Today is Monday
Monday string beans
All you hungry children
Come and eat it up

Today is Tuesday
Today is Tuesday
Tuesday spaghetti
Monday string beans
All you hungry children
Come and eat it up

Today is Wednesday
Today is Wednesday
Wednesday soup
Tuesday spaghetti
Monday string beans
All you hungry children
Come and eat it up

Today is Thursday
Today is Thursday
Thursday pizza
Wednesday soup
Tuesday spaghetti
Monday string beans
All you hungry children
Come and eat it up

Today is Friday
Today is Friday
Friday fresh fish
Thursday pizza

Wednesday soup
Tuesday spaghetti
Monday string beans
All you hungry children
Come and eat it up

Today is Saturday
Today is Saturday
Saturday chicken
Friday fresh fish
Thursday pizza
Wednesday soup
Tuesday spaghetti
Monday string beans
All you hungry children
Come and eat it up

Today is Sunday
Today is Sunday
Sunday ice cream
Saturday chicken
Friday fresh fish
Thursday pizza
Wednesday soup
Tuesday spaghetti
Monday string beans
All you hungry children
Come and eat it up

37 Traffic Lights

"Stop!" says the red light
"Go!" says the green
"Wait!" says the yellow light
Blinking in between

That's what they say and
That's what they mean
We all must obey them
Even the Queen

38 Twinkle, Twinkle, Little Star

Twinkle, twinkle, little star
How I wonder what you are
Up above the world so high
Like a diamond in the sky
Twinkle, twinkle, little star
How I wonder what you are

Wee Willie Winkie 39

Wee Willie Winkie runs through the town
Upstairs, downstairs, in his night gown
Rapping at the windows
Crying through the lock
Are the children all in bed?
I'll have you know it's eight o'clock!

What's the Weather? 40

What's the weather?
What's the weather?
What's the weather like today?
It is cloudy, oh so cloudy
The weather's cloudy today!

What's the weather?
What's the weather?
What's the weather like today?
It is sunny, very sunny
The weather's sunny today!

What's the weather?
What's the weather?
What's the weather like today?
It is rainy, oh so rainy
The weather's rainy today!

What's the weather?
What's the weather?
What's the weather like today?
It is windy, very windy
The weather's windy today!

What's the weather?
What's the weather?
What's the weather like today?
It is snowy, oh so snowy
The weather's snowy today!

41 Wheels on the Bus

The wheels on the bus go round and round
Round and round, round and round
The wheels on the bus go round and round
All through the town

The wipers on the bus go swish, swish, swish
Swish, swish, swish; swish, swish, swish
The wipers on the bus go swish, swish, swish
All through the town

The door on the bus goes open and shut
Open and shut, open and shut
The door on the bus goes open and shut
All through the town

The horn on the bus goes beep, beep, beep
Beep, beep, beep; beep, beep, beep
The horn on the bus goes beep, beep, beep
All through the town

The driver on the bus says, "Step back please!
Step back please! Step back please!"
The driver on the bus says, "Step back please!"
All through the town

The mommy on the bus says, "I love you!
I love you! I love you!"
The daddy on the bus says, "Love you too!"
All through the town

Where Is A-Z?

Where is A?

Where is A?

Here I am!

Here I am!

How are you today sir?

Very well I thank you

Run away, run away

Where is B?

Where is B?

Here I am!

Here I am!

Where is C?

Where is C?

Here I am!

Here I am!

Where is D?

Where is D?

Here I am!

Here I am!

How are you today sir?

Very well I thank you

Run away, run away

(Track 42, sing letters: A, B, C, D

Track 43, sing letters: E, F, G, H

Track 44, sing letters: I, J, K, L

Track 45, sing letters: M, N, O, P

Track 46, sing letters: Q, R, S, T

Track 47, sing letters: U, V, W, X, Y and Z

At the end of track 47, X, Y and Z is sung:

Where are X and Y and Z?

Here we are! Here we are!

How are you today guys?

Very well we thank you

Run away, run away)

48 Zig-Zag

I am a little zig-zag boy who goes this way and that
I never know just where to put my coat or shoes or hat

> I am a little zig-zag girl who flutters here and there
> I never know just where to find my brush to fix my hair

I am a little zig-zag boy who goes this way and that
> I am a little zig-zag girl who flutters here and there
I never know just where to put my coat or shoes or hat
> I never know just where to find my brush to fix my hair

So we are little zig-zag people that's the way it goes
We never know just where to put our brushes or our clothes

49 Zipper Coat

Oh do you have a zipper coat
A zipper coat
A zipper coat
Oh do you have a zipper coat
That goes zzzzip!

Oh yes I have a zipper coat
A zipper coat
A zipper coat
Oh yes I have a zipper coat
That goes zzzzip!

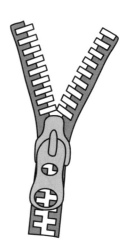